MOSES O OGDENGBE

THE PRICE OF
Destiny

"LIFE IS A GIFT, DESTINY IS A CHOICE."

MOSES O OGDENGBE

THE PRICE OF
Destiny

"LIFE IS A GIFT, DESTINY IS A CHOICE."

MEREO
Cirencester

Mereo Books

1A The Wool Market Dyer Street Cirencester Gloucestershire GL7 2PR
An imprint of Memoirs Publishing www.mereobooks.com

THE PRICE OF DESTINY: 978-1-909874-74-9

First published in Great Britain in 2014
by Mereo Books, an imprint of Memoirs Publishing

The address for Memoirs Publishing Group Limited can be found at
www.memoirspublishing.com

The Memoirs Publishing Group Ltd Reg. No. 7834348

The Memoirs Publishing Group supports both The Forest Stewardship Council® (FSC®) and
the PEFC® leading international forest-certification organisations. Our books carrying both the
FSC label and the PEFC® and are printed on FSC®-certified paper. FSC® is the only
forest-certification scheme supported by the leading environmental organisations including
Greenpeace. Our paper procurement policy can be found at
www.memoirspublishing.com/environment

Typeset in 10/16pt Bembo
by Wiltshire Associates Publisher Services Ltd. Printed and bound in Great Britain by
Printondemand-Worldwide, Peterborough PE2 6XD

THERE IS NO ACCIDENTAL DESTINY;
EVERY DESTINY IS ACTIVATED
BY AN INDIVIDUAL'S CHOICES.

(Deuteronomy 30 vs 19)

CONTENTS

———— ❦ ————

ACKNOWLEDGEMENTS

Nothing of great significance has ever been achieved without the collective efforts of like-minded and inspired people. It was once said, "Without a role model in life, one can hardly play a role effectively". As this book starts from pure inspiration and continues to actualisation, I would like to express my heartfelt gratitude. Primarily to the source of my inspiration, my Creator, for endowing me with the inner strength that sustains and inspires me to come to the awareness of my real identity and functionality.

Next, to all the teachers that have contributed greatly to my life. Some of them are mentioned in this book, but many of them are not. A special thanks to my God-ordained mentor Dr David Oyedepo, whose life and ministry have rejuvenated and transformed my life immensely. I also owe my gratitude to all the known and unknown great minds whose minds I have been privileged to benefit from through books or other electronic means. I am a proof that your legacy lives on.

To my late grandmother of blessed memory, Christiana Mene, a very hard worker who defied the odds of her illiteracy to become a breadwinner. She initiated me early into a life of personal responsibility in my growing days; she taught me the greatest lesson of life, how never to put my hope and trust in people but in GOD. She would always ask me to close my eyes and then open them, and she would ask who I had seen when I closed my eyes. I would answer that I had seen no one, and she would use that to paint the picture of life to me that I have no one but GOD. Her philosophy of life helped me to know the importance of GOD early in my growing-up days. Her wisdom and discipline shaped my life positively.

Finally, to all my friends and well-wishers whose encouragement has played an important part in the pursuit of this work. I acknowledge you all for your belief in me. Your input can never be underestimated; God has really used some of you on diverse occasions to breathe hope into this work. Together we share the success.

DEDICATION

With unfathomable indebtedness and heartfelt gratitude to the Almighty GOD who endowed me with the grace and courage to successfully complete this great work. I hereby dedicate this divine-inspired book to all destiny seekers around the globe, and to my late grandmother of blessed memory, Christiana Mene. Finally to my two wonderful sons, Daniel and Saviour Ogedengbe, who are both my pride and joy.

MISSION STATEMENT

IT'S TIME FOR CHANGE

"It takes a change of mentality to birth a new reality."

There is no genuine change in life that occurs easily. Every true and profitable change is always tied to a cost, which must be consciously paid before one can become its beneficiary.

The change that cannot be first epitomised individually will remain a daydream to realise in any nation. Change is synonymous with the Biblical description of mustard seed, which is meant to evolve from the personal to affect the national.

"Until change is personalised, it cannot be nationalised."

I am one of those privileged individuals who have overcome the hurdles of life. That is why I cannot but utilize my experiences and the grace of GOD that is given to me to serve my generation in the way it should be done. I believe that until we all come to the realization of serving each other according to the gift and the grace of GOD that is given to us, life will remain unfulfilling and cannot be fully maximized. This was the conviction I had within me that made me stand up to the challenge with a belief by divine arrangement and with passion and willingness of heart to reach out to this generation. I want to see the hopeless become hopeful, and also to educate people to the realization of seeing beyond their past and present circumstances in order to gain access and fulfil the ultimate plan and purpose of GOD for their lives. For in every human creature I believe there is a seed of destiny ordained for expression, and because the expression of any seed is in the planting and nurturing, I would like my readers to journey with me as we embark on the exploration of recipe tips for destiny. Also note that I have my own personal passage of life, which I believe GOD is using as the core motivation and passion which are driving this mission.

Remember: The redeemed is ordained to restore, according to Obadiah chapter 1 verse 21, which says, "Saviours shall arise from Mount Zion…"

INTRODUCTION

———◆———

Hebrews 12 verse 2-3 says: "Looking unto JESUS, the author and finisher of our faith, who for the joy that was set before him endured the cross, despising the shame, and has sat down at the right hand of the throne of GOD. For consider HIM who endured such hostility from sinners against HIMSELF, lest you become weary and discouraged in your souls".

There is no glory of tomorrow that will not demand the endurance of today. "Paying for reigning is the rule of life."

The call of destiny will always redefine the course of a man; it can suddenly shift a man from his comfort zone when it's heard and answered. Often times, disappointment happens to man in order for GOD to bring him to an appointment with destiny. It is the interest of destiny that determines how much of GOD any man can experience in the journey of life. Destiny is what validates the right of man's existence, and also the force behind all the experiences we overcome. It is what makes death a no threat to man and the key to triumphant living.

"A man of destiny is an unstoppable entity".

We all have a heritage of golden destiny in GOD. However, we must all pass through the refining fire of that gold in different ways in order for it to be realised. As we all know that the real value of gold can only be realised through the fire of refinement, so must every man allow the refining fire of the circumstances of life to shape his life.

We are either strong or courageous enough to realise the golden destiny, or we remain timid and fearful and jeopardize it.

True glory in life is a journey of diverse tests and trials overcome. No one glory in life can surpass the level of trials overcome. It is in the refining fire of our trials that man's defining moments often emerge in life.

"It takes being persuasive of a future gain to endure the present pain."

The fact that we exist is proof that there is something already completed in GOD's agenda that we are born to initiate. Our existence therefore proves that we are indebted to creation. God has deposited something inside every human which is demanded by creation, and if we fail to disseminate those things, we become robbers of creation, which in effect can cause one's life to start to malfunction.

Failure to comply and contribute to the demands of creation is one of the major reasons why the lives of many are suffering frustration and degradation in our world today. According to the law that governs creation, all creatures are supposed to be interdependent in order to maximize and experience the full glory of creation. However, many have deviated from this set order, which has brought multitudes into self-inflicted suffering.

True living is in the giving of oneself in the area of one's strengths to complement another in the area of their weaknesses. Relevance in life is measured by the joy and happiness that flow through one to others. It is seeking the interests of each other that validates our true purpose of living. The purpose of living is much more oriented to humanity than prosperity. The act of charity is what authenticates any true prosperity in life. The ancient biblical commandment to love your neighbour as yourself still remains the whole essence of human cohabitation. When life is lived in this manner, the prayer for peace will not be needed and the harmony of nature can easily be attracted. True purpose of living cannot be otherwise.

Mother Theresa once said: **"The reason why we are all praying for peace was because we have forgotten that we were created for each other"**. And until we embrace this indispensable truth as our core way of reasoning and living, life will remain an unpleasant adventure.

A wise man once said, **"If you rob a man of his sense of destiny you have destroyed his desire for living"**. This simply means that until destiny is understood, life will remain full of assumptions and manipulations. Where there is no sense of destiny, life becomes a game of trial and error which in effect can lead to miserable and frustrating experiences. Unfortunately this has been the undoing of many in our societies today who have failed to realize that they were born to this world to fulfil a unique and relevant destiny, and this has led to many compromising their uniqueness for a life of mediocrity. It is so sad in our societies nowadays seeing individuals with enormous potential for greatness endangering their lives daily for the sake of survival, when they are supposed to be among the ones dictating the course of events in their generation; this also is a contradiction and an evil under the sun. It will take only the consciousness of our destiny therefore to help us appreciate the purpose and value of living.

"The value of life is measured by the role we play in it."

We live in a world where it is obvious that the value placed on human life has diminished. For example, individuals are killing each other, betraying each other and involving themselves in all manners of evil in order to gain mastery. This is nothing but a result of malfunctioning that is derived from the lost sense of destiny, for where destiny is not understood malfunction is irresistible.

GOD designed everyone for a different destiny, and it is the understanding of this revelation that transforms our perspectives and helps us to be immune to the syndrome of comparison, envy, hatred and all forms of evil that lead to wickedness.

To this effect, true attainment in life can only be a function of fulfilling one's own destiny, which only needs to be discovered and pursued effectively. Then we will realize the old adage that says "Birds can fly together in the sky without interruption". It is only the ignorant therefore who think someone can be an obstacle to their destiny. The ignorance of a man is the strength of his predicament.

For example: Can any beast claim to be an obstacle to a lion in the forest? Such a beast is not yet born; why? Because the lion knew himself as the king of the forest and it is from that consciousness that he derived his superiority, which makes the rest of the beasts in the forest not dare to challenge him. In the same way, once we discover our destiny and begin to walk in the consciousness of it, we also become like lions in the journey of life, and whoever dares to challenge our authority or wants to act as a barrier to our advancement will end up as our prey.

As we all know, the source of anything is also its sustainer. Because GOD is the source and sustainer of our destiny, HE will see to it that nothing can stop us if we compromise not in our relationship and our faith in HIM. Psalm 60 verse 12 says: **"Through GOD we will do valiantly, for it is GOD who shall tread down our enemies."** To this effect it is only where destiny is not known and pursued with faith in GOD that human degradation and depression can emerge.

It is our sense of destiny therefore that motivates us about life; it is what generates our enthusiasm and passion for living, and the source that makes us embrace perseverance in life as the norm. It is the source that gives meaning to life.

The ultimate goal of creation is to make it to destiny. That is why in every human being there is always a deep craving for success, and this craving is what propels all mankind towards the same direction in the journey of life, with the aspiration to become relevant and fulfilled in life. Yet not every aspirant fulfils their goal in life before they die – why?

The reason is because it is often not enough just to be an aspirant in the adventure of life. Rather we must first and foremost be specific and be persuaded of our aspired goal, and then take time to evaluate the demands and the value of that goal in order to know if it is worth pursuing. The more necessary or valuable we aspire to be, the greater our willingness to subscribe to the demand of whatever it takes to accomplish it. That is why to every precious thing in life there is always a price to pay. The prices of such things are always determined by the value that is placed on them, and that value in most instances is determined by its rarity or uniqueness.

So likewise is the mystery of our predestination. We have all been created to fulfil a unique destiny which will validate our value to the world. However, in order to actualize this unique destiny, we must be willing and ready to pay the price that is demanded, because a price must be paid before any goods can be delivered. Therefore to this effect, by the grace of GOD and through the enablement of HIS Spirit, we will be exploring some of the major demands in actualizing a predestined and glorious destiny.

CHAPTER ONE

THE DEMAND OF SALVATION AND SANCTIFICATION

Romans 3 vs 23 says: **"For all have sinned and fall short of the glory of GOD."** *The fall of man was the initiator of life's predicament.*

When Adam and Eve sinned at the beginning of creation, they brought curses both on themselves and on all their descendants to come. We were all embedded in their genetic seed, which is why their sin could affect all mankind. This gives birth to all the evil occurrences that we are experiencing on the Earth today, such as sickness, disease, killing, poverty, mental disorder and every other contrary condition mankind can imagine. None of these were the original intention of the creator. However, in order to be restored to the original state of blessing and harmony which was GOD's original plan and purpose for HIS creation, then GOD in His infinite mercy had to send JESUS CHRIST to die on the cross in our place in order to avert the curse that was inherited through Adam and Eve. Galatians 3 vs 13 says: **"Christ has redeemed us from the curse of the law, having become a curse for us (for it is written, "Cursed is everyone who hangs on a tree").**

Isaiah Chapter 53 vs 5 also emphasises the same: **"But He was wounded for our transgression, He was bruised for our iniquities; the chastisement for our peace was upon HIM, and by His stripes we are healed."** In other words, JESUS wrapped up completely into himself the punishment we deserve, both from our inherited sin and the sin we have committed, and His main purpose in doing this was to reconcile us back to GOD in order to reconnect us back to our heritage of blessing.

Therefore, as we can see, the basic reason behind the struggle and the affliction of mankind can be traceable to the sinful nature that we inherited at the beginning of creation. This has been the principal barrier that has separated mankind from one generation to another for accessing and enjoying the blessing of GOD. Isaiah 59 vs 1-2 says: **"Behold, the LORD'S hand is not shortened, that it cannot save; nor his ear heavy that**

it cannot hear. But your iniquities have separated you from your GOD; and your sins have hidden his face from you so that he will not hear."

Nevertheless, if we are ever going to break that barrier and be reconnected back to GOD in order to gain access to HIS blessing, then we must be ready to possess the sense of reconciliation back to GOD through the medium of salvation by accepting and confessing JESUS CHRIST as personal LORD and SAVIOUR in order for every curse to be averted, then we can re-establish ourselves back into the covenant of blessing.

Galatians 3 vs 13-14 says: **"Christ has redeemed us from the curse of law, having become a curse for us, for it written, "Cursed is everyone who hangs on a tree", that the blessing of Abraham might come upon the Gentiles in Christ Jesus, that we might receive the promise of the Spirit through faith.**

For out of two or three witnesses, the truth shall be established. 2 Corinthians 8 vs 9 also re-emphasises something similar: **"For you know the grace of our LORD JESUS CHRIST though He was rich yet for your sakes He became poor, that you through His poverty might become rich".** As we can see, Christ has already paid the ultimate price for our total liberty from the curses of life that were inherited through sin, so that we can all gain access to the unmerited blessing of GOD. What an awesome privilege.

Romans 5 vs 1-2 says: **"Therefore having been justified through faith, we have peace with GOD through our LORD JESUS CHRIST, through whom also we have access by faith into this grace in which we stand and rejoice in hope of the glory of GOD"**.

It is good to remember once again, as mentioned earlier, that since the fall of the first man in the history of creation the whole generation of mankind has carried the genetic nature of sin irrespective of any self-acclaimed righteousness from any religion which has been set up. To this effect, we cannot afford to remain as ignorant in this dark age of what I called "religious cultism". This is because the greatest source of human manipulation in our contemporary world today can be traceable to this religious cultism, and because too many people's lives have been enslaved and captured by these cults, many believe they can use their avenue as a medium to reconnect back to GOD. They do not know that according to the pre-determined agenda of GOD concerning the restoration of mankind, JESUS CHRIST has been set apart as the prerequisite atonement from the foundation of the world as a lamb that was to be slain for the redemption of mankind and its safety. Revelation 13 vs 7-8 says: **"It was granted to him to make war with the saints and to overcome them. And authority was given to him over every tribe,**

tongue and nation. All who dwell on the earth will worship him whose name have not been written in the book of life of the lamb slain from the foundation of the world".

As we can see from the above scriptures, the matter was decided even before the creation began. However, this also gives us a glimpse of the purpose of the death of CHRIST, which implies that it was not to introduce religion to the world but rather to restore mankind back to our original status as the dominant force on the Earth through a valid relationship with the creator, by destroying the barrier of sin which always denies mankind the access of receiving and possessing the Spirit of GOD, which is also the power of GOD for dominion living.

1 John 3 vs 8b says: **"For this purpose the son of GOD manifested, that HE might destroy the works of the devil."**

To this effect, we must primarily understand that without the shedding of blood there cannot be remission of sin, and this was what JESUS CHRIST did on the Cross of Calvary for mankind, by dying and shedding HIS blood in order for GOD'S mercy to be available to whoever chose to believe and accept what HE came to offer. Salvation through CHRIST therefore remains the primary avenue through which a change of story can commence for anyone that desires it.

1 Corinthians 5 vs 17-18 says: **"Therefore, if anyone is in CHRIST, he is a new creation; old things have passed away; behold, all things have become new. Now all things are of GOD who reconciled us to Himself through JESUS CHRIST, and has given us the ministry of reconciliation."** Consequently, we can see that according to the pre-determined plan of GOD, there is no other name under Heaven by which a person can be saved except that of JESUS CHRIST. Acts 4 vs 11-12 says: **"This is the stone which was rejected by you builders, which has become the chief cornerstone"**.

Nor is there salvation in any other, for there is no other name under heaven given among men by which we must be saved.

This is why the preaching of the gospel of JESUS CHRIST has remained the most potent, current and profitable message of all time. No wonder it is called Good News. It remains the oldest message in the history of mankind without any human review, and is ever fresh in its communication, though in reality, it is much less to the advantage of the preachers that preach it, and much more to the advantage of the hearer who embraces it when is been preached. This is because until we all come to the realization of the mystery behind the sacrificial atonement of the death of JESUS CHRIST, and then embrace it as the only medium of salvation, mankind will keep on being afflicted and frustrated in the adventure of life. That is why the preaching of the gospel of CHRIST cannot be over-emphasised, for it is the power of GOD unto salvation for anyone who believes.

"For I am not ashamed of the gospel of CHRIST, for it is the power of GOD unto salvation for everyone who believes" – Romans 1 vs 16.

SANCTIFICATION

2 TIMOTHY 2 VS 19-21 says:

"Nevertheless the solid foundation of GOD stands, having this Seal: "The LORD knows those who are His," "Let everyone who names the name of CHRIST departs from iniquity."

But in a great house there are not only vessels of gold and silver, but also of wood and clay, some for honour and some for dishonour. Therefore if anyone cleanses himself from the latter, he will be a vessel for honour, sanctified and useful for the master, prepared for every good work".

The above scriptures are a graphic picture of how sanctification determines how useable one can be to GOD, and it also implies how colourful one's destiny can be if it's maintained.

Obadiah 1 vs 17 says: **"But on mount Zion there**

shall be deliverance, and there shall be holiness; the house of Jacob shall possess their possessions."

Just as salvation is all it takes to be delivered and justified from sins and be initiated into a new beginning, sanctification remains the indispensable path to follow in order to arrive at our GOD-ordained glorious end. That is why the Bible says in Romans 8 vs 30: **"Moreover whom He predestined, these He also called; whom He called, these He also justified; and whom He justified, these He also glorified."**

While salvation is the only avenue for justification, sanctification remains the non-negotiable path to follow to glorification. It takes the sanctified to be truly glorified.

The Foundation Of Sanctification

For every destination there must be a foundation. The foundation of a thing is what set the pace for its end; there can be no end to anything in life without foundation. Every starting point in life reflects a picture of an end; foundation therefore is a custodian of any destination.

Every dreadful end in life can be traceable to a bad foundation, while every glorious end can also be traceable to a good foundation. Similarly the quality of our foundation is what defines the quality of our future. What I mean here by foundation does not necessarily imply how we start from our childhood, because those were days of ignorance; rather, it is when we consciously make a decision and start to build our lives for significance. *It is not how far but how well.*

For example, we all know that the fundamental process of any building project is its foundation, and even the strength of that building will also be determined by the depth of its foundation; however, if that foundation is faulty, no matter how attractive the building may look externally after completion it will have no assurance of durability for safety. Psalm 11 vs 3 says: **"If the foundation be destroyed, what can the RIGHTEOUS do?"** To this effect salvation plus sanctification remains the prime foundational demand for every glorious destiny to emerge. The word "sanctification" in our contemporary world today, especially among young people, has become an odd statement which always sounds like a mountain that cannot be climbed because of the immorality that has dominated our world system, but nevertheless it remains the only foundational demand for every genuine enthronement in life. Whenever people hear the words 'sanctification' or 'holiness', the first impression that always seems to come to mind is a burdensome experience. Why? This is a result of immorality in our societies. As a matter of fact it has become the norm in most societies, to the extent that if you claim to be holy or a GOD-fearing person some people will see you as an outcast living in the shadow of civilization. However, it is far better to be an outcast to the world's immorality and its civilization and be acceptable before GOD than to be engrossed and obsessed with the sinful habit of this world which has nothing to offer but destruction at the end.

We live in a world today in which the majority have settled for a mediocre life rather than a life of significance, in order to have the licence of coping with their challenges without endeavour to take the responsibility that will enforce solution. This effect in most cases has turned many to victims of their own undoing, and constrained many to a life of mediocrity.

For example, most people in the journey of life desire the juice of life without being ready to do the squeezing. What many failed to realize is that there must be squeezing before any juice can be produced. Sanctification is one of those indispensable squeezings in the journey of life that can produce the juice which literally means a glorious life. *That is why the word of GOD admonishes us to purge ourselves from every ungodly deed.*

It takes the purging of oneself from every sinful deed to qualify for the outpouring of God's blessing. Besides, there is no true liberty in life that does not always come with burden or squeezing; the truth is that the burden of sanctification is worth bearing because of its amazing benefits, rather than carrying the weight of sin. Sanctification will always promote and enthrone under any circumstances, while sin will always demote and dethrone. Proverbs 14 vs 34 says, **"Righteousness exalts a nation, but sin is a reproach to any people".**

Deuteronomy 30 vs 19 also says: **"I call heaven and earth as witnesses today against you, that I have set before you life and death, blessing and cursing; therefore choose life, that both you and your descendant may live."**

The choice is open to all. For this reason, our foundation through sanctification remains a non-negotiable factor in the pursuit of our destiny, because that is what will determine the level of God's favour we enjoy in our pursuit.

For the sake of emphasis, what is sanctification? It is the purifying of oneself from every sinful way in order to please GOD; it is not a state, as many assume, but a continuous conscious walk with GOD towards perfection. It can also be simply defined as walking in the consciousness of the fear of GOD in all our ways. And the only way this can be achieved is to get acquaintance with the word of GOD and be a practitioner of it, because that is the only authentic source of purification prescribed by the creator. Psalm 119 vs 9 says, **"How can a young man cleanse his way? By taking heed according to your WORD".**

It takes a life of sanctification to be a candidate for a glorious destiny. Every destiny will remain at peril without the foundation of sanctification. Any destiny that is not built on this prime foundation is certain to be devastated at the end; it is just a matter of time. Therefore it is the level of our sanctity that will determine the height of our destiny. However, we must also bear in mind that without a sanctified life no one has a future in GOD. That is why the issue of sanctification remains a non-negotiable requirement for every candidate of a glorious destiny.

Acts 20 vs 32 says: **"So now, brethren, I commend you to GOD and to the word of HIS grace, which is able to build you up and give you an inheritance among all those who are sanctified."** As we can see, it is only the sanctified that are entitled to inheritance in GOD; and an inheritance in GOD simply means a glorious destiny. To this effect we must always strive for a life of sanctity as a way of life, if we desire to be a useful vessel for GOD in executing HIS glorious agenda on Earth in any area of our endowments. Endowment alone does not guarantee a future, it is the backing of GOD that does. Many were endowed in the past and even in our present age and yet disallowed because of their unwillingness for sanctification.

Furthermore, we must also not forget that the whole Earth is groaning for a positive change, and this groaning is a reflection that something needs to be done and GOD is always eager and ready to inject the change, but only on the platform of sanctification. Joshua 3 vs 5 says, **"Sanctify yourselves, for tomorrow the LORD will do wonders among you."** So we can see that in order to experience divine intervention in any deplorable condition, sanctification must take pre-eminence. For anyone to be a candidate of change in this fading world, then the issue of sanctification must also be embraced with all sense of responsibility as an obligation rather than a choice, because without it every destiny will remain at the mercy and desire of the devil, and as we all know that the desire of the devil is that no destiny should see its fulfilment.

John 10 vs 10a says: **"The thief does not come except to steal, and to kill, and to destroy..."** Therefore it will only take a life of sanctity to paralyse all the controlling powers of the devil in the journey of our destiny, this is because light and darkness cannot cohabit; and once we chose to live a sanctify life darkness will give way at ease because sanctity is an enmity to iniquity. John 1 vs 5 says, **"And the light shines in darkness, and the darkness did not comprehend it".**

This subject of sanctification therefore cannot be over-emphasised in the journey of destiny, because without it no one can have access to GOD, and we can all agree that pursuing Destiny without the help of GOD will only end in destitution.

Hebrew 12 vs 14 says: **"Pursue peace with all people, and HOLINESS, without which no one will see the LORD."**

As we can also see, even our access to GOD must be on the platform of holiness, which is synonymous to sanctification. It is the key to every beginning of any glorious end.

Nothing elevates in life like sanctification. It is a multifaceted key that enhances and secures destiny. It is also the key that confers and preserves posterity, and the code that precedes glorification. According to Psalm 112 vs 1-3: **"Blessed is the man who fears the LORD, who delights greatly in HIS commandment. His descendants will be mighty on earth; The generation of the upright will be blessed. Wealth and riches will be in his house, and his righteousness endure forever."**

There is no destiny therefore that can surpass the level of its sanctity. That is why to live an unsanctified life is to automatically register for a dreadful destiny.

The benefits of sanctification are amazing: there are countless benefits that are tied to sanctification, among which is Favour. Psalm 5 vs 12 says, **"For you, O LORD, will bless the RIGHTEOUS; with FAVOUR you will surround him as with a shield."**

It is the favour of GOD that makes the difference in the journey of life, and is behind any true greatness in life. Remember it is not of him that wills, but of GOD that shows mercy. Mercy is synonymous with favour. Therefore every glorious destiny can only thrive on the platform of God's favour, and it takes a sanctified life to attract and enjoy such favour. However, we need to understand that this life of sanctification cannot be achieved in the energy of the flesh; **"For by strength shall no man prevail."** It takes the grace and the enablement of the Spirit of GOD to live a sanctified life in this polluted world.

Zech 4 vs 6 says: **"This is the word of the LORD to Zerubbabel: 'Not by might or by power, but My Spirit,' Says the LORD of hosts."**

This statement of scriptures validates the inadequacy of ordinary mortal man trying to achieve Godly pleasure in the energy of the flesh, not knowing that pleasing GOD can only be achieved by the grace given by GOD.

Philippians 2 vs 13 says: **"...for it is GOD who works in you both to will and to do for HIS good pleasure."**

There will always be contention and resistance against our choice for sanctity, and it will only take the grace of GOD through HIS Spirit to subdue that resistance. Ezekiel 36 vs 27 says: *"I will put my Spirit within you and cause you to walk in my statues, and you will keep my judgement and do them.*" As we can see, it will take the involvement of GOD through the empowerment of His SPIRIT for man to be able to walk in sanctity. That is why it will ever remain a burdensome or unachievable task for any ordinary person that wants to walk in sanctity in the energy of their flesh. To this effect, wisdom demands that we should humble ourselves before GOD with genuineness of heart and motives, and then ask HIM for the Grace required before we embark on it. For it takes only the Grace of GOD for any mortal man to live distinctively in this polluted world. **Salvation plus sanctification therefore remains the foundational demand in fulfilling a glorious destiny.**

CHAPTER TWO

THE DEMAND OF VISION

---⟨⟩---

Habakkuk Chapter 2 vs 1-3 says: **"I will stand my watch and set myself on the rampart, and watch to see what He will say to me, and I will answer when I am reproved.**

"Then the LORD answered me and said: "write the VISION and make it plain on tablets that he may run who reads it.

"For the VISION is yet for an appointed time; But at the end it will speak, and it will not lie. Though it tarries, wait for it; because it will surely come, it will not tarry."

A wise man once said, **"A future that you cannot picture you cannot feature in."**

In the journey of destiny, one crucial demand is the acquiring of vision, either as an individual or a nation; this is because it is the discovery of vision and its effective pursuit that guarantee a glorious future. And this requires us to go back to our creator to seek HIS intention through prayer of inquiry, with all our hearts concerning our existence in HIS agenda on Earth (**see Jeremiah 29 vs 11-13**). It is only from the creator of a thing that the purpose of a thing is made known. And because GOD is our creator, then it is the discovery of what HE unfolds to us in HIS divine plan concerning us on earth that we called "Vision".

For that reason we must first have the vision of where we are going in life or what we are born to do, which is the picture of our tomorrow, before we can successfully embark on the journey of destiny, and this will encompass how to get there, the instrument to get us there, and what must be in place to sustain the vision. For this reason, vision remains the principal force that guides the lives of everyone who would seek a glorious destiny.

In GOD'S agenda everyone is equipped to fulfil a different destiny in life, which is why we have to be genuinely called or assigned by GOD into a specific assignment before we can be guaranteed success. This is because whatever GOD calls for in anyone, He has already supplied, and whatever He assigned us to do, He also designed. GOD will never demand what He never supplied, that is why man's ability is what defines his responsibility. Prominence in life is tied to whatever we are born to do or called by GOD to undertake. We will end up as a mockery and nuisance in any personal ambition we undertake without His consent. GOD is only obligated in backing HIS plan, rather than any plan of man. I understand that many of us might have been driven by our zeal for a particular choice we have once made; nevertheless, we must understand that zeal towards our choice rather than HIS choice can never be a substitute for divine vision, rather, our zeal must be certified and channelled towards our specific purpose in life in order not to be in vain, because zealousness in the wrong direction is sure to end in frustration and vanity.

A wise man once said, **"One of the greatest tragedies in life is to be a success in the wrong assignment". He also said, "The enemy of right is not wrong, but good".**

I believe this phrase calls for sensitivity, because truly the enemy of our destiny indeed knows that if he can succeed in deceiving us to be successful in our personal ambition rather than our GOD'S given vision, he has captured us and he can jeopardize our destiny. That is the reason why we will see many people in our world today busy without being effective, or excelling without making any impact, whereas the ultimate objective in the mind of

GOD concerning HIS given vision is to make an impact and be a blessing to humanity. That is why any vision that is not people oriented or of people's benefit cannot claim to be from GOD; instead it can only be an ambition that is burning with passion, and any ambition and passion that is not certified by GOD can only be an illusion. To this effect our zealousness can only be justified as part of the components that drives our divine vision to fulfilment.

"Pursuing God's plan guaranteed safety, while personal ambition makes one vulnerable to the wickedness of man."

Until we have a clear vision of our specific assignment in life, the journey of destiny can be very frustrating and unfulfilling. For if we study carefully the problems of some individuals and nations in our world today we will discover that some of these problems can be traceable to lack of vision or lack of clarity of vision. This happens even in the so-called developed nations, where we have leaders who have no clear picture of the destination to which they are leading their nation and citizens to. As a result they become frustrated, unfulfilled and victimized by all manner of contrary circumstances. Why? This is because having no clear vision of where we are going in life can make one become a wanderer, going through life aimlessly, hoping for all things and ending with nothing. Proverbs 29 vs 18a says:

"For where there is no vision, the people perish".

Therefore vision remains one of the fundamental requirements for the realization of any destiny either as individuals or nations.

CHAPTER THREE

THE DEMAND OF PRAYER

James 5vs16b) says **"The earnest (heartfelt, continued) prayer of a righteous man makes tremendous power available (dynamics in its working) "The art of prayer is the source for spiritual empowerment"**

Prayer is the generator of power that gives motion to vision for the actualisation of destiny; it is a spiritual missile that disarms every unseen obstacle in the journey of destiny. We must spend more time on our knees in prayer, if we are to continue walking in power. A prayer less individual is a powerless entity in the journey of life.

Vision of Destiny may be likening to a spiritual pregnancy conception, while Prayer is the spiritual force that births the delivery. It takes travailing in the labour room of prayer to birth a prevailing Destiny in life. (Isaiah 66vs8) says, **"Who has heard of such a thing? Who has seen such things? Shall the earth be made to give birth in one day? Or shall a nation be born at once? For as soon as Zion travails; she gave birth to her children"**. Here is a synonymous pictorial picture of the mystery of travailing prayer for delivery. The scripture above shows us how travailing in prayer is paramount to any delivery of vision and destiny. That means Destiny could be stagnant without prayer, and because every vision of Destiny is a spiritual conception, therefore, it will take the force of prayer to enforce its delivery in the physical. "Prayer is the source of spiritual empowerment to reign in the physical."

(I Corinthians 16vs9) says, **"For a great and effective door has opened to me, but there are many adversaries."**

From the above scripture, we also realised that every open door or any pursuit of relevance in life will always attract adversaries. The fact that we have a sure Destiny in GOD does not mean that the enemy will not contend, however, we must be able to have what it takes to subdue him. That is why Prayer is a vital force to engage for combat in the journey of Destiny. It is the medium of generating power from above. No matter how great a Destiny may have been predestined, without prayers, it will lack the power for realisation. This is because Prayer is the link that connects humanity to divinity for any earthly interference and productivity. (Psalm 2vs8) says, **"Ask of me, and I will give you the nations for your inheritance, and the ends of the earth for your possession."**

Even though Destiny may be reveal through vision, GOD still wants us to remain connected to him in prayers for seeking counsel and intervention against any confrontation and obstacles in our journey. Maintaining regular union with God in prayer therefore remains a vital demand for the realisation of any predestined glorious destiny.

We live in a world full of cruelty, where every good intention is always opposed and challenged. (Psalm 74vs20) says , **"Have respect to the covenant; for the dark place of the earth are full of cruelty".** To this effect, Prayer has been ordained as an avenue to seek and cry out to GOD for justice over any hindrances to our destiny. Our predestined destiny is a covenant between us and GOD, and prayer is the prescribed platform to keep reminding God of this covenant whenever we are challenge or confronted by circumstances. Destiny will always attracts both known and unknown battles into our lives, which is why we cannot afford to be prayer less in our destiny pursuit. Prayer is a necessity in the journey of Destiny; it reveals the dependability of man on His source which is GOD, and because without the aid of the source, no destiny can be resourceful. It is via prayer therefore that we remain connected to our source.

Prayer is also a platform to seek an aid for supernatural transformation of Destiny. (1 Chronicles 4 vs9-10) says , **"Now Jabez was more honourable than his brothers, and his mother bore him in pain." And Jabez called on the GOD of Israel saying, "Oh that you would bless me indeed, and enlarge my territory, that your hand would be with me, and that you would keep me from evil, that I may not cause pain!" So GOD granted him what he requested.** The art of prayer is a medium for supernatural turn around. Destiny could be contested, but it takes engaging the force of prayer not to be defeated. Destiny is simply a call into a battle of a predetermined victory. However, it takes individuals battle mentality approach in prayers to appropriate such victory.

(Deuteronomy 2vs24) says I quote, **"Rise, take your journey, and cross over the River Arnon. Look, I have given into your hand Sihon the Amorites, King of Heshbon, and his land. Begin to possess it, and engage him in battle".**

Here is a graphic illustration of how what has already been given could still demand our engagement in battle

(prayer) before actualisation. Prayer is a weapon of warfare, in which we engaged in order to appropriate our predetermined victory in life. (2 Corinthians 10vs3-5) says I quote, **"For though we walk in the flesh, we do not war according to the flesh. For the weapon of our warfare are not carnal but mighty in God for pulling down strongholds, casting down arguments and every high thing that exalts itself against the knowledge of GOD, bringing every thought into captivity to the obedience of CHRIST"...**

It has once been said that a closed mouth is a closed Destiny, and I believe there is an element of truth in that saying, because there would always be some confrontation of different kinds on our way to destiny, and the only effective way to overcome these confrontations is by engaging the force of prayers. Destiny is a journey of warfare that demands a warfare mentality approach, while Prayer is the spiritual missile for dislodging every attack on the way. In every man's promise land, there are evil resistance, which is why the subject of Prayer cannot be over emphasis because it is a spiritual weapon for combat in any pursuit of relevance. A prayer less approach to destiny will always lead to destiny casualty; there is nothing of great value in life that is casually achieved. **To this effect, the demand of prayer remains a vital force** to engage for the realisation of any glorious Destiny.

CHAPTER FOUR

THE DEMAND OF RESPONSIBILITY FOR PRODUCTIVITY

———◆◆◆———

Destiny is designed by GOD, but it takes man's responsibility to define it.

Isaiah 6 vs 8 says:

"… Also I heard the voice of the LORD, saying: Whom shall I send, and who will go for us?" Then I said, "Here am I! Send me."

"You may not be responsible for your place of birth, but you will for your place in destiny"

"Until we learn to embrace responsibility in every given opportunity, the universe will remain infertile to our desire expectation".

A wise man once said **"Any faith that holds GOD absolutely responsible in the affairs of man is an irresponsible faith."**

This simply means that GOD will always involve man in the implementation of any of HIS plans on Earth, either for a revival or revolution. For example, in the ancient days, when the children of Israel were in captivity under the oppression of Egyptian dictatorship and GOD decided to deliver them after HE heard their excruciating cry of injustice, HE never came down from heaven. Rather HE sought a man called MOSES to represent HIM see **(Exodus 3 vs 7-10)**. Also when HE wanted to avenge the Jews against the plot of Haman, HE positioned Esther, one of the Jewish descendants in the palace of the King, as a Queen, and used her to procure favour in the sight of the king **(Esther chapters 5 & 6)**, and finally when HE wanted to save the world from its chaos under the domain and influence of Satan, HE never send an Angel; rather, HE sent JESUS CHRIST in the form of a man (see **John 1 vs 1-13**). And even in the contemporary world that we all live in today, all the scientific inventions and technology, and all other essential things that have made living more comfortable for mankind, were not directly made by GOD; rather GOD packaged all in the form of ideas and dreams and invested it inside mankind. Then through divine inspiration mankind took responsibility by using their initiatives for innovation to produce all that has added more glamour and comfort to creation today. Therefore as we can see, man will always have a role to play in GOD's agenda as a vessel concerning any change of situation on earth. This is because from the beginning of creation GOD has assigned all earthly affairs to the care of man. Genesis 1 vs 27-28 says: **"So GOD created man in HIS own image; in the image of GOD He created him; male and female He created them. Then GOD blessed them, and GOD said to them, "Be fruitful and multiply; fill the Earth and subdue it; have dominion over the fish of the sea, over the birds of the air, and over every living thing that moves on the Earth."**

Psalm 115 vs 16 says, **"The heaven, even the heavens, are the LORD'S; but the Earth HE has given to the children of men."**

Man was originally appointed to manage all earthly affairs on behalf of GOD; however, GOD still remains the owner. To this effect every candidate of destiny must awake and arise with anger from his or her laxity and rediscover their true function over the affairs of life. When a man is convinced of his purpose and future, he begins to confront and challenge the fear of his past and present. For this reason, I believe the due time has finally come for us to manifest our true callings in order to inject the positive changes needed in our generation, as we all know that true liberty demands both personal & national responsibility if we are ever going to make any difference in our lives and in the lives of others. We must understand that our refusal to change for the betterment of our future will only make us remain in the captivity of our past as destitute. A wise man once said: **"Anyone that will not apply new remedy must expect new evil to emerge."** As we also know, we have been enslaved for a very long time by the common saying "Whatever will be will be", which, I believe we can all agree, has not proved itself.

To this effect, I want us to know that life will never grant us what we desire. rather, it is what we angrily demand from it that we will get by subscribing to the demands of life through embarking on the race of personal and national responsibility. Anger is an element that GOD has deposited in us to use as an enforcer of our desired change in life. Anger is a virtue, if it can be appropriately used in a just cause. Until we become angry with our current predicament and embrace the garment of both personal and corporate responsibility to devise a way of enforcing a change, things will remain as they were.

The desire of man not only depends on GOD; every true desire in life is always tied to a definite decision of man. Life revolves around the cycle of human daily choices, and until those choices are appraised and changed, the cycle of our current episodes will continue to prevail. Our mentality must be reawakened from its passivity about our contrary state and we must decide to take our destiny in our own hands, if we don't want to become a mockery to our critics. GOD has done all HE could; we are only responsible for what becomes our portion by the choices we make and pursue. Our destiny is in our hands, let's wake up to it.

Martin Luther King Jnr said, **"Liberty is never given voluntarily by the oppressor; it can only be demanded by the oppressed."**

For this course, we need to all awaken from our slumber and subscribe to this only avenue of responsibility that can make our lives more meaningful, because we must never mistake our contrary situation for our portion. However, it will only take a genuine response against our contrary circumstances to enforce our desired change. Every change of position in life will always demand a repositioning. And we need also to realize that we cannot derive more from life than we invest in it.

This is why I am convinced that we are the only ones that can enforce the positive change we desire, by beginning to take personal responsibility for our lives in cultivating and developing our individual gift, and in using it to serve and add value to each other and to humanity. GOD designed our destiny and gave us the gifts to take us there; nevertheless it is how responsible we are in cultivating those gifts and their implementation that will determine our profiting in life. The truth is, until we define our true life direction and surrender ourselves completely to it, life will continue to resist our demands. To this effect it is time for us as individuals to begin to search and look around our environments and societies for any unwanted situations that our gift can match for solutions. This is because the key to every solution in life is in the implementation of the gifts that God has endowed each one with. Inside every problem around us is concealed the opportunity to attain stardom in life. And until we begin to see life from that perspective and learn to approach it with the same mindset, we cannot really maximize our potential and get the best out of life. For where there are problems, there is wealth in a potential form.

GOD does things in a mysterious ways, and he always hide fame and wealth inside problems and expect His people to discern it and turn it around for their own advantage.

"It is the glory of GOD to conceal a matter, but the glory of kings is to search a matter" (Proverbs 25 vs 2).

We are all surrounded by opportunities that are packaged in the form of problems in all our environs, but only those that can discern and maximize them can become the beneficiaries. However, we cannot be a problem solver, until we are first a student of problems; our business world of today was born out of studying problems. If we can successfully study a new problem, we can create another new successful business. What the poor see as problems and challenges are the makers of the rich. The difference between the rich and the poor lies in their perception of things. Wisdom demands that instead of spending our time waiting for opportunities to come our way, we should be investing our time in searching and looking for problems we can solve with our gifts and talents. Though God considered necessary the prosperity of His people, however, it takes the problem-solving ability of individuals to appropriate his or her portion (**see Deut. 8 vs 18**).

GOD wouldn't have endowed us with gifts or ability if there was nothing to use it for. A gift is essentially for profiting, if only it can be maximized. I discovered in my search that there is nothing mystical about being great in life. From my personal discovery and point of view, I believe that the secret to greatness is simple: just be a solution provider and you will become sought after, irrespective of your CV or background.

Responsibility simply means to respond with our GOD endowed ability to life opportunity around us.

Life is like a blank cheque book given to everyone to write their personal worth in it, and the only pen that can write in that cheque book is the pen of responsibility. The blessings of life are allotted to individuals according to the level of their responsibility in the area of their gifting and callings.

"Life will only respond to what we are worth, not what we want".

The world has heard enough of complainers; they are eagerly waiting for the changers. Therefore GOD has placed a demand on every one of us in every area of our individual gifting in order to enforce the changes needed in our societies and nations.

Romans 8 vs 19 says: **"For the earnest expectation of the creation eagerly waits for the manifestation of the sons of GOD".**

By virtue of predestination, GOD has deposited a seed of greatness inside every individual in the form of a gift. Romans 11 vs 29 says, **"For the Gifts and calling of GOD are irrevocable."** And it is in cultivating that gift and in using it to serve our world in positive ways that we will make the greatness in us emerge, which in effect will culminate in our significance in life. Proverbs 18 vs 16 says:

"A man's gift makes room for him, and brings him before great men."

So until we deploy ourselves to serving our individual gift to each other and humanity, life will remain unfulfilling. This is one of the main reasons why so much blame and pressure has been heaped on the government for lack of employment, just because we have been refusing to deploy ourselves to our individual's gift, which is one of the major ways we can eradicate unemployment in our nation and bring fulfilment to everyone.

Consequently, if we refused to deploy ourselves to our gifts, someone else will keep us on the track of employee and this will continue to generate dissatisfaction among us. I am very much aware that in life there is always a time to be an employee or apprentice for the sake of learning and gaining experience which is normal. Nevertheless, deployment of gifts still holds the key to true satisfaction in life.

It is only in the area of our gifting that we can derive true fulfilment, and besides, no employers can truly pay our true worth in life. Everyone's true worth is hidden in their inherent gift, which must be cultivated and deployed before it can materialize.

We need to also understand that it is when we excel in the area of our gifting that we can attract the attention and command the respect of people, even if they don't like us.

It was George Washington who once said, **"Excellence is the cure for racism"**. That simply means that our exceptional attainment in life through our positive input is the only way to silence our critics. Our gifts therefore must be traded with excellence if we must command the envy and silence every critic of our destiny. To this effect deployment remains the answer to both personal and national satisfaction. **"It takes being productive to be resourceful."**

The value of a thing will always be hidden if it is not explored or discovered. That is why I am fully persuaded that our value as a person or nation can only be found in the revelation of our destiny, which demands our personal responsibility to discover. Until we discover the value of a thing it will remain irrelevant, and in order to be relevant in life, which was God's original plan and purpose for every human being, then we must all crave to step out from the shallowness of trusting in man or believing in the government for our fulfilment in order not to violate the commandment of GOD. According to the original plan and purpose of GOD, mankind was wired and designed to be absolutely dependent on GOD for instruction and direction in order to be fulfilled in life. That is why the word of GOD says in the book of Jeremiah (17 vs 5-8) that **"Cursed is anyone that put his trust in a man and makes flesh his strength whose heart departs from the lord"**.

Life is governed by a simple yet unnoticed truth called "thought". The power of one's thoughts is the power of one's life, and every human, irrespective of race or colour, lives in the world of their thoughts. Every circumstance of man is a consequence of his thoughts and beliefs, not government or background. Therefore pointing the finger of blame is nothing but ignorance of TRUTH. No one can be liberated beyond their thoughts in life. True liberty can never be given by any human; it must be realised within oneself, or it is fake. The greatest discovery in the history of mankind is not of gold or diamonds, but of self-discovery. When our thoughts set us free, life and circumstances have no choice but to harmonise us. In the adventure of life, we conquered more by positive thoughts than any human technique. To this effect I believe it is time for us to re-orientate our mentality in order to change our perspective towards life.

Every change in life begins with a change of perspective, and until we re-orientate our mentality to match the expectation of our creator, life will remain a burdensome adventure.

Truly when we look at the problems that are facing the world today, it is very obvious that the world is in urgent need of solutions. However these solutions, according to most people's views, are the need for the right governmental system, and the misconception of these views has been the cause of the long-time deplorable condition of many nations, even in the developed world. Yet the more they call for changes in government the more they realize that the problem remains unsolved, and they get stuck in the circle of confusion. The truth of the matter is that the real solution to these problems is beyond what any governmental system can really solve. That does not deny the need for the right system, but before we can start to seek the right government, I believe the mental re-orientation of the people is of utmost importance, because until we interrupt our habitual way of thinking and form the right way, even when the right government emerges we might find it difficult to recognize and appreciate it.

The subject of change is more needed in our individual mentality of today than even in our governmental set-up. This is because we are more often the victims of our own personal misconceived ideas and beliefs than our circumstances, and until the liberation begins from our mindset we may never experience the liberty of true living.

All true and profitable liberation in the history of mankind has always begun with man's reorientation of mentality. Real change is more a matter of the right mindset than the right government. Therefore I believe it is time to begin to challenge our present philosophy for the sake of the incoming generation and also for the betterment of our own future.

Personally, I believe that there is nothing wrong with any nation, irrespective of any contrary situation that may be affecting their citizens. However, I believe that every affected citizen in any nation is nothing but a victim of their own wrong philosophy and ignorance. The cause of every negative scenario in life has its origin in either lack of knowledge or misconception. This is because it is possible to be in a nation with good administration and full of opportunities and still end up as a victim when one is operating and living by the wrong philosophy. This wrong philosophy in most cases might have been a result of misconception in the early stage of our lives; nevertheless there is still a way out, if only we can admit it and be ready to reprogram our mindset. Misconception is one of the greatest tragedies known through human existence, and it has subtly destroyed many glorious destinies. To this effect, our current wrong philosophy must be altered if we are to recapture the original concept of life and wish to become the beneficiary of its treasures. This is the reason why the mental conversion of the people remains the fundamental requirement for the maximization and appreciation of any right governmental system.

God is much more interested in a change of man's perception than his condition. It is often a change of perception that affects a change in conditions. Most human struggles require more reorientation than intervention.

Romans 12 vs 2 says: **"And do not be conformed to this world, but be transformed by the renewing of your mind, that you may prove what is that good and acceptable and perfect will of GOD."** So the right thinking of the people remains one of the major demands in transforming any society or nations.

It should be noted that we have to also understand that it is the company of great people that can make a great nation, and it will also take responsible citizens to produce a responsible leadership. To this effect we cannot afford to be wasting our time relying on governments for the changes we desire, because this will never change anything. Rather it is the personal development and the general input of the citizens that will. And until we start to work on ourselves in order to achieve the changes we wish to see, we cannot be their beneficiaries.

Change in life is essentially more about who we become than what we experience. It is time therefore to stop putting our hopes on the vain promises of governments if we truly desire genuine and profitable change. This is because there is no governmental system that can really guarantee a positive change; it is an illusion to live by. Rather, a change is something we can only attract by the person we all become individually.

So working on ourselves to attract positive change remains the most profitable adventure that one can embark on in the journey of life. There is a seed of change embedded in every human; any change of circumstances in life will always require a changed personality. True and lasting change is the attraction and reward of a changed life. A change must first be epitomised before it can affect its surroundings.

Archbishop Desmond Tutu said, **"We must not allow ourselves to become like the system we oppose."** This implies that the only way to move forward in life, regardless of any contrary circumstances, is to personally initiate desired change, and then constructively address all the unwanted circumstances in our lives in order to create a better future. Change is a personal choice. That is why every engagement today, either consciously or unconsciously, is a seed for our future harvest.

In the words of Dr Fredrick K C Price, **"If we fail it is our fault and if we also succeed it is our fault."** That means we did something to make things happen. So the destiny of any individual or nation can only be a function of both their personal and national responsibility.

According to the demand of life, every human being is expected to define their destiny through personal responsibility. In the book of Proverbs 6 vs 6-11, the word of GOD painted a graphic picture of an ant as an example of what we can emulate:

"Go to the ant, thou sluggard! Consider her ways and be wise, which having no captain, overseer and ruler, provide her supplies in the summer, and gathers her food in the harvest. How long will you slumber, O sluggard? When will you rise up from your sleep? A little sleep, a little slumber, a little fold of the hands to sleep, so shall your poverty come on you like a prowler, and your need like an armed man."

It is very clear from the above statement what lack of responsibility can generate. We all need to realize that until we start to make a move individually and corporately nothing will ever move, because every exploit in life is a product of an adventure, and there is also a physical law that says, "Every object will remain at a state of rest until a force is applied to it". To this effect there must be an enforcement of any changes we desire, either as individuals or nations, in order to see its actualization. It has been said that the best way to predict the future is to create it.

I also understand that most of the people in the world today have been engaging in one prayer or the other to GOD for solutions to their deplorable state of being; this I believe is the right approach, because truly it will take divine intervention to turn any contrary situation around. However, we must not forget that we have a role to play, and that the GOD we are seeking is a responsible GOD, who will only answer the prayers of people who are ready to take responsibility for their lives. **"When we refuse to do what is expected of us by HIM, it makes our prayer lives of no effect".**

Life is designed to be lived by principles, not by miracles, according to the plan and purpose of the Creator. So waiting for miracles without applying the principles will only keep one on the dark side of life. We don't wait for miracles rather; we work them out by engaging their principles. There is principle behind the order of every happening in life. It is applied principles that bring true and lasting miracles from obstacles. Compliance to God's instructions and principles therefore is the only valid way to accelerate the delivery of any man's desire and expectation.

When we learn to obey and concur with God's demands, it helps to pray less and generate more positive effects in life. "Prayer may deliver, but it takes responsibility to be an achiever in life".

The desire of man is not only dependent on GOD; every true desire in life is tied to a definite decision of man. Until we reawaken our mentality from being passive about our contrary state and decide to take our destiny in our own hands, life will keep on challenging our belief. God has done all he could; we are only responsible for what becomes of our portions. Therefore, if we truly desire divine intervention in any deplorable state, then one of the familiar ways that GOD answers prayers is by showing the revelation of what to do, sometimes through divine ideas that will bestow responsibility on us, so as to create the changes we desire. And until we act on whatever HE reveals to us, we cannot experience HIS act. Psalm 103 vs 7 says, **"He made known HIS ways to Moses, and HIS act to the children of Israel".** So we can see that it is HIS ways that always precede His act, and His ways are simply responsibilities placed on man. GOD will never violate HIS principles for anyone except those that align themselves to his ways; besides, we need to also remember that GOD never promise HIS blessing based on nothing, rather HE promises it based on the works of our hands. Deuteronomy 28 vs 8a says, **"The LORD will command the blessing on you in your storehouses and in all to which you set your HAND."** Every promise of GOD is a responsibility placed on man.

There is always something we can do in order to see HIS acts see (**Deuteronomy 28 vs 1-13 and Exodus 23 vs 25-26**). It is our practical engagement therefore in whatever GOD has revealed to us that will attract HIS blessing in our direction.

To this effect, it is easy to identify the reason why idleness has remained the major cause of the present deplorable condition of some individuals and nations. It was Albert Einstein who said, **"The world is a**

dangerous place, not because of those who do evil, but because of those who look on and do nothing."

We live in a world today where everything is changing and failing, and even the governments of nations are confused. For example, in the western part of the world, which we call civilized, civilization has become the enemy of their wisdom, through which the pollution of intellectualism has damaged the belief system of the citizens, and this is gradually causing their formal glory to fade. There is nothing wrong with civilization if moral perception is maintained and sustained. However, no one can claim to be more civilized than GOD, the creator of mankind and the entire universe, because what we called civilization is basically an opening of eyes to a new facet of life, and the same is what GOD did in the beginning of creation, when HE turned what was meant to be a dark world into the planet where we all reside. But unfortunately the counterfeit civilization of man has offer less positive benefits than negative ones. This same civilization has presented the devil and his agents with the avenue to implement their evil mission on mankind, by subtly allowing mankind to keep living contrary to the law that governs their make up for the sake of temporary pleasures. This has destroyed many destinies in our so-called civilized world of today.

To this effect, I would like to admonish everyone,

especially those in the other parts of the world which the wisdom of man has categorically classified as "third world nations", and say that they were right, it has never been their fault – rather, it has always been our fault, because ever since the colonization we have been made to believe that we are not valuable because of the historical mental damage which the oppression of colonialism had caused to our mentality and personality. This has led to their discernment of our poor and unproductive thinking, which some of us have grown to believe and accept. Nevertheless, the verdict has been overturned, so we must allow a shift in our way of thinking. **We are not what we are called until we agree.**

What classifies a man as a third world citizen is neither his geographical location nor his colour of skin; rather it is his state of mind and the inability to use his mind productively in order to become what GOD has destined him to become. That is why I am convinced that what makes a man or a nation rich or powerful has nothing to do with possessions or natural gifts but has more to do with the ability to use his mind to cultivate, replenish, be fruitful and also to dominate, which was GOD's original intention for every man on earth irrespective of race or location **(see Genesis 1 vs 28).**

According to GOD's original agenda, man was designed and created to use his mind to get the best out of life, which is why for example we see people that have no natural resources in their native country travel to another country to purchase resources cheaply and then use their brains to transform the resources into finished products, then sell these products back to the original owner of the resources at a price which is ten times more than he was given for it. We can see that the reason why they called us third world nations was because they knew we were ignorant of what it takes to become a first world nation through the inability to use our minds productively in order to get the best out of what GOD has already endowed us with. This is why I believe a change in our thinking and living is needed now more than ever before, if we are ever going to be truly fulfilled and to realize our true potential as individuals or nations. To this effect, creativity among the individuals within a nation remains one of the cardinal avenues in creating a developed and prosperous nation.

It takes the involvement of every individual in a nation to form the total development of that nation, which is why in order to make the changes we have been seeking and wanting we must begin to take responsibility personally and nationally in activating our minds for creativity, because the success of any individual or nation can only be a function of the productive use of their mind.

It has been said that the wealth of this world is not from

the oil of Kuwait, nor from the diamonds of South Africa or the gold of South America; rather it is all conceived in the minds of individuals, in the form of dreams and plans that will need to be executed before they can be realized.

The mind of a man is the fountain of his blessings, if it can be put to work. It is the greatest resource that GOD has given to mankind, not natural resources.

Human resources have remained the greatest asset of all developed nations. Every advanced nation in the world today is built on the platform of creativity which is a function of the productive minds of its citizens. The United States of America, Japan, China and South Korea are among the nations that have attained their global recognition and stardom through the use of their human resources for creativity. For this reason creativity remains one of the cardinal demands for every individual and nations to experience advancement and progression in life.

No one can progress beyond their creative instinct in life.

CHAPTER FIVE

THE DEMAND OF RIGHT MOTIVE AND INTEGRITY

———◆———

1 Samuel 2 vs 3b says: "For the Lord is a GOD of knowledge; And by HIM actions are weighed." "The motive of a man is his real identity."

Nothing in life is worth aspiring to unless it is inspiring. Motivation is the soil upon which any seed of aspiration must be planted. Nothing can be genuinely called good until the motivation behind it is pure and right. Good is often known more by motives than deeds, while intention is also more essential than decision in the adventure of life.

One of the vital areas where we need to constantly examine ourselves in the journey of our destiny is in the area of our motives and integrity, because these might as well be another hindrance to our advancement if they are not properly appraised. We need to understand that until there is a change from within, there cannot be a change from outside. That is why we cannot but make sure that we maintain good conscience and integrity in all our endeavours, both as an individual or nation, in order to live a successful and dignified life. It is also good to note that in the journey of destiny these two factors must also be maintained and sustained if we are to keep enjoying the backing of the ALMIGHTY GOD in all our affairs.

Psalm 50 vs 3b says: **"…and to him who order his conduct aright I will show the salvation of GOD."**

For that reason we must be ready to fight anything that may want to contend against our destiny, either through the corruption of environment or society. We must understand that every suffering we endure for the sake of the truth has greater rewards to follow. **(See Matthew** 5 vs **10-12.)**

So let us not be afraid to pay the price of whatever it takes to maintain a good conscience and integrity in the journey of our destiny, because when destiny calls we must have courage to answer. This is why it is mandatory to make integrity in our lives the foundation of our living. Nothing protects and preserves like integrity. Every seed of integrity that we sow today will surely yield a harvest of dignity and honour tomorrow. To this effect, let us radically break loose from the captivity of corruption and enter into the ark of integrity, which is capable of saving us from the danger and the calamity of what corruption leads to.

I believe that many of us were once victims of corruption in one area or the other in the past, but that does not deny the effect and the efficacy of integrity, because the people who said "no" to corruption in the past are the ones who are fulfilling destiny in a colourful way today. Destiny is a race of patience and perseverance, any attempt to run it otherwise could lead to a miserable end. Every destiny is wrapped up in a set time. There is no short cut in life; every short cut will always leads to a short life. Jeremiah 17 vs 11 says, **"As a partridge that broods but does not hatch, so is he who gets riches, but not by right; it will leave him in the midst of his days, and at the end he will be a fool."** For that reason let us learn the lesson of life from life itself.

I do not really believe that we have any special problem other than the problem of ignorance, which I genuinely believed was the main reason behind the destruction of many destinies in our world today. No wonder the word of GOD in the book of Isaiah 5 vs 13a says, **"therefore my people have gone into captivity because they lack knowledge".**

"Ignorance is the greatest unnoticed destroyer of mankind."

My mentor Dr David Oyedepo once said: "There is no problem anywhere that every man's ignorance is his problem" (I paraphrase). To this effect, I believe that if we can all seek and embrace the TRUTH, which is the word of GOD as the foundational guide for our living without any compromise, then we shall all break loose from that yoke of ignorance which has destroyed the lives of many, and we shall also be establish in righteousness which will grant us access to the blessing of GOD, and make HIS glory to reflect in every of our endeavour. Then we will all realize that nobody should determine our value; rather we shall be the one determining our value to the world through the use of our mind in productive ways and our doctrine of integrity, which will enhance our value and become a characteristics that will form in us a Godly character which no mortal man can gainsay nor resist.

CHAPTER SIX

THE DEMAND FOR CHARACTER DEVELOPMENT

"The real growth that brings one to prominence in life is not the growth of age, nor of stature, but of a sound character."

You might ask, what is character development? It simply means to undergo a process of mental, emotional toughening through perseverance in order to become a predictable and reliable person.

The prime factor in the journey of destiny is actually not in how one arrives, rather, it is the sustainability of that destination that really counts, and this can only be achieved by a sound and mature character. Any attainment that we cannot maintain and sustain in life will hold no lasting significance. Besides, we all know that in life there are many crooked means that people go through to attain prominent positions; the sustainability of that position in challenging times is what will prove the legitimacy of the occupant. This is because whatever does not have a genuine foundation cannot stand the test of time.

It was Dr Martin Luther King Jr who said: **"The ultimate measure of a man is not where he stands in moments of comfort and convenience, but where he stands at times of challenge and controversy."** This is why I believe the subject of character development is pivotal in every aspect of life. I strongly believe it is one of the major missing factors in our societies and nations today. Most people in our societies, especially our leaders, seem to be professing what they are not, and this has led to catastrophe in many societies and nations. Most of the so-called leaders in our contemporary world are nothing but professional manipulators. It takes character to be an effective leader, and once this principal factor is lacking, they begin to manipulate and pretend to be good leaders. For this reason I believe it would be better as an individual or nation not to pursue any ambition or goal in life that is beyond the capacity of what our characters can match and sustain, because whatever our character cannot match and sustain is not worth having. Any aspiration that is beyond the strength of one's character can be suicidal to one's destiny. This is because we live in a world today where we have over-celebrated skills, talents, anointing, power and all other attribute of success we can imagine, but one thing we have failed to realize is that as precious as all these gifts and attributes are, without character they will amount only to vanity and mockery in the end. This is because character is the shield that protects every gift and destiny.

The effects of lack of character can easily be seen in most of our governmental set-ups of today, especially in the seats of power where we have leaders who are deliberately violating the constitutional rights of their citizens without any sense of guilt. This has becomes the norm in most nations and has resulted in dreadful conditions and the abuse of many people's destinies. Where there is no display of character, chaos is the immediate outcome. And if any leader of any nation or organization lacks character it will automatically affect the status of their followers.

To this effect, it would be advisable for every incoming leader in any human endeavour to make character development rather than degrees and talents their utmost priority before they aspire to any prominent position. The prospect of every individual and nation can only be maintain and sustained by the solidity of their character. However, it is important to note that character cannot be learned from any institution, nor can it be attained through any level of academic qualification - it can only be developed through experiences such as trials, pressure and the challenges of life that we endure and overcome through faith and perseverance.

Romans 5 vs 3-4 says: **"...and not only that, but we also glory in tribulations, knowing that tribulation produces perseverance; and perseverance, character; and character, hope."**

For that reason, I urge anyone who wishes to fulfil their destiny to face the challenges and trials that are presently confronting them with perseverance and faith in GOD, and this will in turn develop the character which will enable them to withstand the test of time when charting the course of destiny. To this effect, it is time to awake to the call of redefining the destiny of our generation in order to move from obscurity into the liberty that was once established, which we have long ignored, so that we may start living and stop just existing. Life was designed to be enjoyed and not to be endured, according to the original plan and purpose of the creator.

CHAPTER SEVEN

THE DEMAND FOR DIVINE WISDOM

———⟨❦⟩———

Proverbs 4 vs 7 says, **Wisdom is the principal thing; therefore get Wisdom. And in all your getting, get understanding."**
"It takes the wise to rise and shine in crisis."

One of the purposes of a crisis is the revelation of the wise. God always uses crises to distinguish the wise from the unwise; wise people are those that see a crisis as an opportunity to reign.

In life there is what is known as major and minor, and one of the major demands to actualize a glorious destiny in life is divine wisdom. It takes the operation of this major weapon to overcome all the obstacles and manipulations of the opposition. It is the master key in the school of life. However, it is interesting to note that there are different types of wisdom in operation in our contemporary world today which was listed in the book of (**James3 vs 15-17**) the earthly wisdom which can be call common sense, the sensual wisdom which can be call intellectual wisdom, and the demonic wisdom which refer to the occultist, sorcerers and diviner. But there is one left that is called the wisdom from above, which is divine wisdom.

Someone may ask, how can one know the difference? Divine wisdom simply means the knowledge and the application of scriptural (biblical) principles, or walking in the understanding and reality of scriptural (biblical) precepts.

Every other wisdom can only at best make us smart. Only divine wisdom can truly make us wise in the affairs of life. The real issues of life are far beyond what any smart individual with his wisdom can overcome. We reign in life through divine wisdom (**see Proverbs 8 vs 15**). Divine wisdom is what validates true smartness in the adventure of life. Walking in divine wisdom is therefore the most authentic path anyone can follow in creating an enviable future.

I believe we are in an era when people of no significance in the past are gaining recognition and stardom via the channel of taking personal responsibility for their lives, which connotes the principal responsibility of recognizing the source first, which is GOD, and then returning back to him in total and absolute submission in order to gain access to HIS wisdom for transformation and revolution. It is only the wisdom of GOD that can answer the hard questions of mankind and deliver them from all abuse and destruction. For this reason, we all have to return to the wisdom of ages of our Covenant fathers Abraham, Isaac, and Jacob, because the divine wisdom these individuals exhibited during their lifetime was what guided their lives and made them generational icons.

Nothing dignifies destiny like operating in divine wisdom. It remains the principal virtue that births any glorious destiny. One cannot operate in this principal virtue and not reflect heavenly glory on earth. It is the secret behind every extraordinary accomplishment in life. Matthew 11 vs 19b says: **"And God's wisdom is justified by results".** This is why we need to stop believing and trusting only in our intellectual wisdom, because I believe this has turned our world today into chaos. The problems that are facing our world today are far beyond what any intellectual mind can comprehend or solve. Isaiah 29 vs 14b says: **"For the wisdom of their wise men shall perish, and the understanding of their prudent men shall be hidden."** To this effect I believe it is time to redirect all our hopes and focus back to the supernatural wisdom of GOD, the creator for total solution, because until we admit that we need help and for

GOD to intervene, life will remain chaotic and mankind will continue to suffer from its ignorance and rebellious lifestyle.

That is why the word of GOD admonished us in the book of 2 Chronicles 7 vs 14:

"If my people who are called by my name will humble themselves, and pray and seek my face, and turn from their wicked ways, then I will hear from heaven, and will forgive their sin and heal their land." Therefore we must be ready to admit that we are limited in the knowledge we need to find solutions to our present chaotic situation, and we should cry out to GOD the creator that knows the end from the beginning and seek HIS wisdom for our total liberation.

It is the endowment of this divine virtue that gives value to our spirituality and determines our worth in life. Whatever good we become in life is a product of the level of this kind of wisdom at work in our lives. It is the builder of every unique and glorious destiny. No wonder the book of(James 1 vs 5 says, **"If any of you lack wisdom, let him ask of GOD who gives to all liberally and without reproach, and it will be given to him."**

CHAPTER EIGHT

THE DEMAND FOR SENSITIVITY AND ENDURANCE

A wise man once said, **"A person that cannot see the ultimate will become a slave to the immediate"**.

I strongly believe that the above quote is synonymous to what many destinies are undergoing in our world today; the inability to visualize the future from the present, thereby giving the opportunity to the manipulators to take advantage. To this effect, we must all be very sober and vigilant in watching out for the destiny manipulators who are going around taking advantage of people's ignorance in their deplorable state by offering them temporary comfort for permanent solutions in order to rob them of the glorious days ahead. When the victims cannot see what the manipulator can see, they become the victim of their own sightless tomorrow in their present painful experience. They forget to understand one of the principles of destiny that says, **"Every weight of glory will be preceded by a season of affliction and trials."**

Therefore we must not be afraid to pay the price of endurance today as we pursue the vision of our destiny and also in walking upright before GOD; this is because all the trials and challenges in the journey will all be forgotten on the feast of our destiny. Let us not look at the way we are today to judge our tomorrow, because whatever we can see today is liable to change. This is the reason why we must all be the followers of those who through faith and patience obtained the destiny they foresaw.

However, we must also realize that GOD always plants a big dream in a small or unrecognized vessel, because HE doesn't want us to live by what we see, rather HE wants us always to live by faith in order that He may turn impossibilities in our lives into possibilities so that people will know, acknowledge and adore HIM in our lives as the only source of every good and great accomplishment. (**See Hebrews 10 vs 38 and Habakkuk 2 vs 4**)

We must bear this in mind that the realities of life will always challenge our faith in the journey of our destiny. However, we must learn to ignore them and set our focus only on the unseen realm of all possibilities with our eyes of faith in GOD, if we desire to see the fulfilment of our destiny.

"It takes focusing on the invisible to defy the odds of impossibility."

"Destiny signifies the terminal, while faith in GOD is the driving force that take us there."

Let us take a look at some of our past and present heroes who paid the price of destiny in the past to achieve God's plan for their life and the life of their nations, such as Martin Luther King Junior. He was pastor of a nice church in Alabama and one day when the black people in America were still slaves to the white Americans he saw a vision for equality. This became his passion and conviction, and when people saw this it inspired them, and they allowed him to influence them to the extent that he ordered almost half a million people to walk from Alabama to Washington. Why? Because he saw that one day his people would no longer be judged by the colour of their skin, rather by their character. We have seen all that came to pass in the life of first black American president in the person of Barack Obama. But we must not forget that it took self-sacrifice and some years for the vision to be accomplished, because the passion and conviction of his vision became an obligation that set him on a course of self-sacrifice that influenced a change in the fundamental law of America.

Another example is Dr Nelson Mandela. Dr Mandela

was just an ordinary person like us, a young lawyer by profession, until one day this young man caught a vision of destiny for freedom and the vision became an obsession for him which led to his arrest. Yet he remained convinced about his vision, and that compelled him to pay the price of being imprisoned for 27 years. Why? Because he chose to pay the price of seeing the realization of his vision, rather than surrender to the temporary torment of the opposition for the sake of his destiny and their nation. Destiny can never fail unless we faint in the pursuit. Even in jail Mandela's persistence and endurance shocked the entire world, and men and women in all walks of life began to support him by all available means in the realisation of his dream for South Africa. On his release from prison the whole world saluted his courage and tenacity. Today we are all living witnesses to the reality of that vision that took him from prison to the presidential palace and ended apartheid. Today Nelson Mandela is a name in the world of politics recognized as an outstanding African legend.

So let us not sell our destiny cheap under any circumstances because of affliction, or any temporary contrary circumstances that might blindfold us not to see an opportunity in opposition or a gain in a painful experience.

"If only we could allow the pains of our lives to drives us towards a change, we could end up become the heroes of our world."

CHAPTER NINE

THE DEMAND OF DIVINE GUIDANCE AND DISCIPLINE

———— ❧ ————

"Divine guidance is the gateway to man's distinction"
"It takes someone that can see ahead to lead ahead"

One of the greatest tragedies in life is to know where we are going and not know how to get there, this can be very frustrating and can make one to become impotent or dormant in the journey of life, which in effect can also derail one's potential and jeopardize ones dream.

It is interesting to note that no mortal man has the capacity to lead himself according to his divine make-up. Proverbs 16 vs 9 says: **"A man's heart plans his way, but the LORD direct his steps."**

Therefore our greatness in life can only be a function of divine guidance. However, it will be a dangerous thing to succeed in life without divine aid; this is because every success in life will always attract envy, and because envy is the beginning of wickedness, and where there is no divine aid wickedness will always prevail. To this effect, no human effort can be a substitute for divine guidance in the journey of destiny. It is what makes the journey of destiny easier, and also the mystery that covers all our weaknesses and reveals our brilliance in the journey of life.

"It takes being guided by God to be shielded from evil."

In pursuit of the vision of our destiny, our undying and unwavering commitment is also crucial. By this I mean believing in our vision with all our hearts, which calls for a lot of discipline, focus and most importantly following divine guidance, because only those that are focused, disciplined and led by GOD in the pursuit of their vision will end up being distinguished. However, taking short cuts in life has been the undoing of so many people and nations and has caused so many disappointments and so much decadence. To this effect we will have to always be divinely guided in the journey of life in order not to miss our place in destiny.

You may be thinking, what is this divine guidance? It is simply the communicating of the mind of GOD to us through our spirit or our heart for direction in order not to be victimized in the journey of life; we can simply call it the spiritual navigator of destiny.

We can all agree that it takes someone who knows the way to show us the way, and because GOD is the custodian of our destiny who gave us the vision to pursue, HE is the only one who can also guide us successfully to the realization of it, because only HE knows every end from every beginning. Isaiah 46 vs 10 says, **"I make known the end from the beginning, from ancient times, what is still to come. I say: my purpose will stand, and I will do all that I please."**

My mentors once said that one wrong step in life can wreck a whole destiny. That is why there cannot be a substitute for divine guidance in the pursuit of vision and destiny. To this effect how much of the divine guidance we hearken to will determine the level of the victory and glory we can experience in the journey of our destiny. This is because only following divine guidance can ensure our victory over all opposition in the journey of our destiny. For this reason, divine guidance remains one of the master keys for the fulfilment of any glorious destiny. Without it vision and destiny are vulnerable to oppression and destruction.

One major fundamental requirement for accessing and enjoying this divine guidance is meekness, which simply means to be gentle in nature and easy to lead. However, we must also remember that being meek does not necessarily mean that we are weak; it simply connotes dependability on GOD for judgement. Psalms 25 vs 9 says, **"The meek will he guide in judgement: and the meek will he teach HIS way".**

This statement of scriptures shows us that God does not lead and guide everybody, only those that are meek in nature. Therefore until we are free from pride we cannot qualify for HIS guidance. To this effect we must learn always to humble ourselves and acknowledge GOD in all our endeavours in order for HIM to always direct our path, because we must realize that not every opportunity in life is of GOD; many are traps in disguise. So it takes meekness to walk with GOD in order to ascend our throne in destiny. Proverbs 3 vs 5-6 says **"Trust in the Lord with all your heart, and lean not on your own understanding; in all your ways acknowledge HIM, and HE shall direct your path."**

ILLUSTRATION

The story of the first American billionaire in history, John D. Rockefeller, is a typical example of the efficacy of meekness and divine guidance. When his organization bid to provide insurance for the *Titanic* and later won the bid, the Spirit of GOD told him not to go for the deal and he obeyed, despite the fact that the ship was unsinkable, according to human experts. He chose to be guided by

GOD through his meekness rather than trusting in the verdict of those human experts, and ended up escaping the unforeseen disaster that was ahead. If it had not been for his meekness in following divine guidance, that would have been the end of the John D. Rockefeller empire. Today his foundation organization is still blessing humanity just by being led by divine guidance. Proverbs 14 vs 2 says, **"For there is a way that seems right to a man, but its end is the way of death"**.

DEMAND OF DISCIPLINE

A wise man once said **"Destiny is the source of both personal and national discipline."**

It takes the knowledge of the glory that resides in our future to discipline ourselves today. It is essential to note that discipline is one of the major hallmarks of a glorious destiny. It simply means to put oneself under a certain rule in order to get the best out of oneself. It can also be defined as going the hard way now in order to avoid a hard life in future. It is the force that keep destiny on track.

The journey of destiny can be likened to a marathon race which is governed by certain rules and regulations. As we all know, it takes discipline to abide with those rules and regulations in order not to violate them and experience their consequences. Likewise in the journey of destiny; we are all in a race that is governed by principles and it is abiding with those principles that guarantees our success. 1 Corinthians 9 vs 24-27 says, **"Do you not know that those who run in a race all run, but one receives the prize? Run in such a way that you may obtain it. And everyone who competes for the prize is temperate in all things. Now they do it to obtain a perishable crown, but we for an imperishable crown. Therefore I run thus: not with uncertainty. Thus I fight: not as one who beats the air. But I discipline my body and bring it into subjection, lest, when I have preached to others, I myself should become disqualified."**

So as we can see, anyone who wants to embark on the journey of destiny must be willing and ready to subject themselves to the demand of discipline. The issue of discipline in the pursuit of destiny is not negotiable and it must be practised with all sense of responsibility if we are to arrive at our glorious destiny.

Until we win the war of personal discipline, destiny will remain a day dream. Personal discipline is the indispensable way of accomplishing any glorious thing in life. That is why we must all embrace it as a lifestyle in order to enjoy an enviable future.

If we refused to discipline ourselves, life itself will discipline us in a hard way and this might not be a pleasant experience. Therefore if truly we desire to experience the national revival we have been longing for, the demand of personal discipline must be embraced by every individual, not as a choice, but as an obligation. This is because it is our personal discipline that will give birth to national discipline, which will in turn culminate in national resurgence. **Therefore discipline remains one of the major demands for the actualization of any destiny.**

CHAPTER TEN

UNDERSTANDING THE PURPOSE OF AFFLICTION THROUGH OPPOSITION

A wise man once said, **"There is no danger in having opposition, it is only dangerous not to identify it."**

"The knowledge of our opposition's weakness gives us an advantage to device and implements our winning strategies".

It is important to note that every good course in life is heavily contested by many seen and unseen forms of opposition, even in the journey of destiny. 1 Corinthians 16 vs 9 says, **"For a great and effective door has opened to me, and there are many adversaries".**

Whatever will take us to our peak in life will first and foremost attract some critics in the form of opposition.

According to Dr Myles Munroe, **"If the purpose of a thing is not known, abuse is inevitable"**.

One of the greatest tragedies in life is to have the wrong concept about something. This is why I believe a good understanding of what affliction, emanating from opposition, symbolizes in the individual's or nation's destiny will help us to position ourselves and prepare us adequately when opposition arises. GOD will sometimes reveal the picture of our destiny to us through dreams and visions, which come in phases, and has bestowed on us the responsibility for accomplishing it. And inside every vision of destiny lies the means to pay for its accomplishment, which sometimes symbolizes affliction that emanates from opposition. This also comes to challenge the fruition of our vision and destiny, and this affliction that emanates from the opposition often connotes among other thing discomfort and rejection. That is the reason why I believe we need the proper comprehensive meaning of what affliction symbolizes in the journey of an individual destiny or nation, because some people believe that all affliction is a result of sinful ways, not knowing that some afflictions are permitted by GOD for a particular purpose in the life of an individual or nation. However, we must also understand that every affliction of life is common to all men, and there is always a way out. 1 Corinthians 10 vs 13 says,

"No temptation has overtaken you except such as is common to man; but GOD is faithful, who will not allow you to be tempted beyond what you are able, but with the temptation will also make the way of escape, that you may be able to bear it".

For maximum understanding, let us now look at some examples of individuals and nations that were afflicted for some particular purpose.

The story of Joseph in the Bible was a typical example. Joseph was a teenager when he had a dream and saw the vision of his destiny as a ruler, and when he saw it, he was so excited and impressed that he could not keep it to himself. He explained the vision to his father and his brothers. Out of envy they all disagreed with him, without any of them knowing what GOD had packaged together as the components and plans that would bring about the fulfilment of the vision he saw in his dream. Why? Because GOD knew that if Joseph saw the plan he would be afraid to pursue his destiny, because inside the plan lies the price to be paid for the accomplishment of his destiny. This symbolizes affliction, which is also contrary to Joseph's expectation and philosophy about life, and those affliction connotes discomfort, opposition and rejection in order to explore in him the character required to have dominion over the challenges that await him in his destiny. But one vital question we need to ask here is what Joseph did wrong to deserve all the trials and tribulations he went through? Absolutely nothing, but it pleased GOD to explore and refine the leadership seed that was hidden in him. However, it was Joseph's fear of GOD and his faith in GOD that empowered him to overcome all those afflictions. That is why Joseph could boldly declare in the end that all the afflictions he went through, GOD meant it for good purpose for his destiny.

No wonder the word of GOD says in the book of Romans 8 vs 28-29 **"that all things works together for the good of those who love GOD and are called according to HIS purpose." Vs 29 says for those GOD foreknew HE also pre-destined."** So from the word of GOD, we can see clearly that sometimes predestination can be the cause of our past and present circumstances, even as we have seen from the life of Joseph.

Let us look at Israel, as a nation that was also afflicted and greatly opposed without her consent. Before Israel came into existence, her destiny and afflictions were also predetermined by GOD for the purpose of their destiny (**see Genesis 15 vs 13**). Why? Because it is only the manufacturer of a product that knows the purpose of his product and for that purpose to be accomplished, he must make sure that the product is tested and proved before it is released for its purpose. Because Israel was destined to inherit the land of Canaan as an inheritance, a land that was flowing with blessings without any of their effort, and GOD knew that it would be very difficult for them to manage and sustain the land because they didn't work for it, we must also understand that it was supposed to be their inheritance according to their destiny so they did not have to work for it. That was the reason why GOD predestined their affliction and their discomfort in order to train them for discipline and develop the character that would be needed in them when they arrived in their Promised Land for maintenance and sustenance.

For further illustration, let us consider someone who leaves a multinational company to his unborn child as an inheritance, and the child is brought up without any form of education in running a business. We all know the child will automatically mismanage and ruin the business, much to the dissatisfaction of his father, because he has not been trained with the knowledge and character required to manage and sustain it. Afflictions and opposition among many other things sometimes train us for discipline and stretch our capacity to comprehend all that life is about, because from the word of GOD we discovered that not all affliction is as a result of waywardness, rather some affliction and opposition is designed and permitted in the lives of some people to refine and purify them for the purpose of their destiny. That is why we must always learn to be sensitive and patient in affliction, because sometimes GOD uses affliction to develop the character of an individual or nation, even as we have seen in the life of Joseph and the nation of Israel.

"GOD will only commit HIS treasures to the hands of those that have passed the test of life through a season of affliction and trials."

Psalms 105 vs 19-21 says, **"Until the time that his word came to pass, the word of the LORD tested him. The king sent and released him, the ruler of the people let him go free. He made him lord of his house, and ruler of all HIS possessions."-**

Nevertheless, we must also understand one of the principles of destiny which says, *"Whatever GOD demands HE will also supply"*. Therefore if GOD permits any affliction or discomfort as a test in the life of any individual or a nation for the sake of their destiny, HE will also grant them sufficient grace to overcome those afflictions. For the will of GOD will never takes any man to where HIS Grace will not protect them. That is why the word of GOD says in Psalms 34 vs 19 **"Many are the afflictions of the righteous, but the LORD will deliver him out of them all"**.

From this point of view we can all fully understand that afflictions can

be experienced even by the righteous, and this gives us

a clear perception that not all afflictions of life are a result or consequence of sinful living.

ILLUSTRATION

May I refer to the true-life story of one of the largest supermarkets in England, where I have worked for a couple of years. Marks & Spencer was founded in 1884 by a man of Jewish descent called Michael Marks. He had escaped persecution by the Russian Government territory in Poland to come to England. When he landed in Hartlepool in the North East of England, he had nothing, and slept on the floor of a synagogue (Jewish church); he could not even speak any English. But he came with an endowment of imagination and spirit, and after a long period of struggle and discomfort which symbolize affliction, he ended up meeting Thomas Spencer in Leeds by divine arrangement. Spencer was born and brought up in England and was also endowed with tenacity and persistence. They would never have met had it not been for the persecution (which represents affliction) which compelled Michael Marks to leave his comfort zone to travel to an unknown land. Of course, they ended up as one of the most famous business partnerships in English history.

After all their journey of struggle and change they both had children, who were still very young when their fathers died. But before they died they had brought some intelligent minds into the business for progress and stability, and some of these later became shareholders in the company.

When the children attended their first company meeting they did not attend as directors, rather as shareholders with their parents. When they were growing up, one of them, Simon Marks, foresaw the destiny of the company and realized that if he was ever going to ever secure control of his late father's business, he would struggle to manage it because of his lack of experience in business, even though he had just finished a grammar school education. He also realized that he had limited knowledge of the world and he knew clearly that he had to possess qualities of character and will, as well as intelligence and imagination, if he was to succeed in securing the control of the business, which he later paid for and acquired. That helped him to secure full control of the company's destiny. Thomas Spencer Junior, however, lacked the qualities of his late father and he refused to pay the price of acquiring those qualities that would have empowered him to fight the battle for the control of the company's destiny. He was later pushed out of the business, except for the royalties he received as a shareholder.

As we can all see from all avenues of life, there is always some price to pay if we are ever going to be in charge in life either as an individual, nation or business. That is why the price of destiny must be paid with all sense of responsibilities in order to become what GOD has destined us to be, either as an individual or nation.

Responsibility remains the ultimate price for greatness.

CORRECTION

Let us now explore the other phase of affliction for clearer understanding. A wise man once said that **"Sincerity does not necessary mean that we are always right; rather, it is being able to be corrected when we missed something that validates our sincerity."**

This kind of affliction, as we all generally know by common definition, is anything that torments or generates discomfort and distress in the life of a person or nation. A person or a nation can also be afflicted through their sinful and rebellious lifestyle. Affliction can also be used as a correction rod between a sheep, which symbolizes a person or nation, and GOD, who symbolizes the shepherd. It is sometimes the correction method that GOD uses to teach His rebellious children obedience. This is because the sheep do not always go in the direction the shepherd wants, and the shepherd has the responsibility to bring them back on track. Sometimes it can be the shepherd using his rod which symbolizes affliction if the sheep are unyielding. We all know that a sheep can never lead itself to a destination without the shepherd; this is why we must all embrace the affliction of life sometimes as a correction to our waywardness.

I believe that inside every affliction of life there is usually some hidden knowledge to explore. Psalms 119 vs 67 says, **"Before I was afflicted I went astray, but now I keep your word." Vs 71 says, "It is good for me that I have been afflicted, that I may learn your statues."** By this I am convinced that I have painted a comprehensive picture of what affliction symbolizes in the life of both the righteous and sinner, and also what it can become if we hearken to correction and choose to be in right standing with GOD through CHRIST. Therefore let us sometimes see the affliction of life in a positive way either as a correction, rather than a destroyer of destiny, especially if we are privileged to be in right standing with GOD through CHRIST.

No matter what the circumstances of life throw at us on the way to our destiny, GOD is always aware of it and HE has equipped us with what it takes to overcome them. For GOD is the sculptor of our lives and destinies. HE constantly remoulds us as HIS dear children to fit the purpose of his agenda, sometimes by allowing discomfort and unpleasant experiences on our journey to destiny, so as to form in us the mature character that will be needed for the stability of our dominion in future. It was C.S LEWIS that once said, **"Hardships often prepare ordinary people for an extraordinary destiny"**. Therefore if we are ever going to fulfil destiny, we must all be committed followers of GOD and HIS ways, because it takes the leadership and guidance of GOD to accomplish a glorious destiny.

JESUS IS LORD

www.ingramcontent.com/pod-product-compliance
Lightning Source LLC
Chambersburg PA
CBHW060031050426
42448CB00012B/2957